FRENCH HOME COOKING

Savory Secrets from the Heart of France
(2023 Guide for Beginners)

Benedict Silva

CONTENTS

Home Cooking in France

Introduction

French cuisine is renowned as the foundation and core of many delicacies worldwide. In reality, the history of cuisine can only be understood by considering how French cooks influenced a big chunk of our current history. The strength and appeal of French cuisine are legendary, and it has gained the reputation of being elegant and sophisticated. Techniques utilized in French cuisine are extensively taught in modern culinary programs and cookery instruction. In actuality, Le Cordon Bleu in Paris, France, is one of the world's most well-known and highly regarded cooking schools.

French cuisine ranges from rustic, woodsy foods to complex, exquisite dining and everything in between. Northern France is at one end of the spectrum, with vineyard crushing, salt production, and slow-roasted stews. The other end of the scale is the Parisian custom of elevated dining: rich candies, gold-brushed croquembouche, pickled cucumbers, and thick roux. In addition to visual appeal, French cuisine strongly emphasizes flavor and spice. The Pyrenees produce flattened red Espelette peppers, and the Region of Biscay salt mudflats are covered in fleur de sel flakes. Even in the South, vineyards produce some of the best wine and liquor in the country. Furthermore, Provence's lavender fields and olive groves can be found far further along the Mediterranean Sea.

Although the French are known for their culinary prowess, there is no need for French cuisine to be fussy. The heart of French cuisine is to highlight new, high-quality goods so that their fundamental flavors and formulas stand out. Of course, butter, milk, cheese, and other culinary minefields are staples of French cuisine, but they don't have to take over the plate. It was discovered that French cuisine could be relatively healthful. France is one of the world's healthiest countries, with small portions and a focus on healthy living. Aside from its rich gourmet food, France is abounding in healthful meals.

"French Home Cooking" is a recipe book in French. It is divided into four chapters that examine French cuisine in-depth and include all recipes. The first chapter provides a quick overview of French food and history. The chapter also discusses historical facts and regional impacts. The second chapter contains recipes for breakfast and snacks. The third chapter discusses the main entrees for lunch and dinner. In chapter four, you'll discover some delectable dessert and bread recipes. Begin reading the book right away and get ready to prepare delectable French cuisine to spice up your day.

Chapter 1: A Quick Look at French Cuisine

The heart and soul of many Western cuisines were known as French food and preparation. The influence and love of French cuisine cooking methods are legendary. That importance is precisely why learning French cuisine can be intimidating for a beginner. Many cooks believe they must conform to an unattainable standard of beauty and elegance in French cuisine.

Because the impact of traditional French cooking is delicious, the basis and many other delights are widely referred to as French food and cuisine. French cuisine may appear sophisticated, but it is about preparing a cohesive meal, such as Burgundy's coq au vin. You can learn how to make vinaigrette in a specific approach so that once you have perfected the salad, you can seek one of the most straightforward recipes nearby, like a poultry brag that is all soft and tender within.

Different courses of French feudal meals can be cooked but devoured simultaneously.

The liquids were dark, sweets were popular, and buttercream pie was invented in the Middle Ages. Northeastern France today has a surprising range of flavors, focusing on apples, bacon, and pork. Metro France's residents are multi-cultural but also make traditional French cuisine with fresh fruits, gratin verts, mushrooms, or dried fruits. They would typically create local dishes, gaining a strong sense of territoriality. Chicken and sheep, which are especially plentiful from early fall through February, are available all year, but France has a surplus.

1.1 The Intriguing History of French Cuisine

In the Middle Ages, the history of French food began with the explanation of culinary contracts and concise recipes.
However, let us skip the Dark Ages and consider some of the revolutionary improvements that occurred following the Revolution to understand better how French cuisine originated in history. Until the fifteenth century, when sugar mania seized the country, French recipes were typically acidic--sugar in water, vinegar, fish, and pork! Later in life, this practice resulted in a significant shift in French feeding

patterns: a clear line was drawn between sweet and salty meals, and sweets were often presented at the end.

French cuisine served as a model for other cuisines in the seventeenth century. To begin with, this century has seen people begin to feed with a fork! While forks were popular in places like Italy, the French believed forks were stupid and ate with their hands for years. Intellectual debate and reading have become a big topics in France. The cuisine was portrayed as an aesthetic medium and contested in peace, science, and religion during the Revolution.

By the end of the eighteenth century and well into the nineteenth, "cuisine bourgeoise" recipe books had grown relatively popular. This dish developed court-served aristocratic cooking, usually chocolaty, rich in meat, and spices, and cooked for periods in boiling jus (flavors). Local foods such as boeuf bourguignon, bouillabaisse, coq-auvin, and gratin dauphinoise, as well as mother roux sauce, are examples of this meal. In comparison, the French Revolution sparked the collapse of the guild members, which was a watershed moment in the food business. With guilds no longer operating, French chefs might manufacture and sell any food commodity they pleased. This resulted in a kind of awakening within the French food industry. More gourmet professionals are discovering new routes for various recipes and meals.

French cuisine has lost part of its global hegemonic status.
Numerous exciting outsiders to the worldwide fine dining scene have outperformed the current French chefs. The triumph of modern French cuisine is not unimportant.

1.2 Historical Information and Traditional French Cuisine

Herbs, plantains, and mushrooms were unpopular in France.
Until the fourteenth century, seasoning mixtures and designs were popular. France had a lot of farm food; it was simple food with no frills. In the middle of the fourteenth century, Catherine de Medici returned to Florence to meet Crown Prince Henri II, bringing with her Florentine-educated cooks and a love of aesthetic drama and decorum. In the coming years, French cuisine will evolve into a

significant art form with magnificent looks and inventive flavors.

The nineteenth century brought about significant changes in French cuisine. The intricate preparation of global food has made it popular, and the detailed exhibition is modern haute cuisine. It was the French food processing model before it was criticized by critics for being overly rigid. The current cuisine reacted to the classic strong French cuisine of the 1970s. It lightened the cream sauce and utilized fewer ingredients to focus on the true taste. It is visible in today's distinctive French cooking through various preparation processes and increased experimentation with non-traditional variations.

Each person consumes an average of 46 pounds of cheese every year. French cuisine is a unique gastronomic experience that mixes elegance, leisure, medical preparation, and spicy, healthful meals. Producing and preserving French food is a craft that takes years to master but also requires time to enjoy. Begin investigating and accepting French cuisine as an art, a discipline, and a way of life.

France offers a different cheese for every day of the year. Food is a fundamental priority in traditional French society. The French consider eating to be not only neutral but also a tradition. People in France frequently drink hot liquids from cups and drop bread or pastry into them. France became the world's first country to prohibit stores from discarding unsold produce to prevent food waste. Instead, it is contributed to charities and other programs by shops. France produces 10 billion baguettes per year. In France, over 500,000,000 snails are consumed each year. A standard baguette should only have three ingredients: wheat, yeast, and spice. It must also weigh 260 grams.

1.3 French Food Specialties by Region

Typically, the French bake and cook recipes from their nation.
This is not to say that they are provincial; the French have a great sense of elegance, which is why urban French cuisine in France is alive and well. In urban France, they will likely sample a diverse selection of national and regional dishes. This is true worldwide, where people are multicultural or from several ethnic groups. Traditional French dishes

are heavily used in local goods. New grapes, haricot verts, chives, mushrooms, squash, and dried fruits are among the most popular goods. Year-round, chicken, lamb, beef, and veal are readily available, and during the hunting season, which runs from early fall to February, animal flesh is abundant. No matter where you go in France, you'll find abundant artisanal wine and cheese.

Southern France features the rich, exquisite flavors of mushrooms and ducks and the dramatic spices, peppers, and olives introduced from surrounding Mediterranean cuisines. Northern France also has a diverse array of tastes, focusing on farmhouse-style occupations involving grapes, milk, cattle, potatoes, bacon, and beer. Traditional French culinary products and cooking methods vary widely across France. Each region has a distinct and distinctive cuisine based on the various customs and prepared dishes that have evolved in France.

Chapter 2: Recipes for French Breakfast and Snacks

2.1 Recipes for French Breakfast

Cafe au Lait in French

Time to cook: 7 minutes
Serving size: 1

Ingredients:
⅔ cup milk
2 tbsp ground coffee
⅓ cup of water

Method:
1. Process and prepare coffee in a coffee machine.
2. Warm the dairy on the stovetop or in the oven to froth the dairy, then pour it into a French press.
3. Use the plunger to withdraw hot milk until it rises in length.
4. The simplest and easiest technique of frothing milk at home is to use an electronic dairy frothier that warms and foams at the same time.

5. The drink pours equal parts coffee and dairy, allowing you to customize it to your liking.

Easy French Chocolate Cake

Time to cook: 13 hours and 10 minutes
Size of each serving: 16

Ingredients:
1 to ½ cups chilled whole milk
1 semi-sweet 4-ounce bar
2 tsp sea salt
1 tablespoon dried active yeast
¼ pound unsalted butter
granulated sugar ¼ cup
4 cups regular flour

Layer of butter
1 big egg
2 tbsp full-fat milk
2 tbsp. all-purpose flour
The egg wash
1 ½ oz. unsalted butter

Method:
1. Cut the butter into four 1-tablespoon pieces and place a food processor fitted with the dough hook in the pan.

2. Stir in the rice, salt, and yeast. Switch the machine to higher speeds for two minutes to gently combine the components.
3. While the machine is running, slowly pour in the milk.
4. Turn on the machine and pound the flour for at least five minutes, or until all of the milk has been applied.
5. The dough will be light and fluffy. If you poke it with your palm, it will pull away from the container walls and bounce right back.
6. Remove the bread from the pan and shape it into a sphere with lightly oiled hands.
7. Remove the dough from the oven. Begin flattening the dough with your palms.
8. Transfer the mixture to a prepared baking sheet or a baking sheet covered with paper towels.
9. Place the entire sheet pan in the fridge for thirty minutes to cool the buttered surface.
10. Place the folded dough on a rimmed baking sheet and cover with bubble wrap or plastic wrap for 4 minutes to cool.
11. Shape the croissants.
12. Preheat the oven to 204 degrees Celsius.
13. Combine all of the ingredients for the egg wash.

14 Remove the croissants from the oven.
Clean each one lightly with egg wash.
15. Bake for 20 minutes or until the
croissants are golden brown.

Omelette française

Time to cook: 15 minutes
1 serving size

Ingredients:
ground black pepper, freshly ground
1 tbsp. unsalted butter
2 teaspoons milk
a pinch of kosher salt
2 huge eggs

Method:
1. In a large mixing bowl, combine the egg
whites, milk, spice, and seasoning and mix
well with a spoon or a fork.
2. Place the sheet near the burner.
3. Preheat a thin omelet tray or a nonstick
saucepan over medium heat.
4. When the pan is hot, add the butter.
5. Sprinkle the oil in the saucepan while
it heats.
6. Add the eggs once the butter is
scorching hot and the bubble has subsided.
7. Using a heat-proof spoon, stop to allow
the eggs to warm slightly before whisking

vigorously, making sure to use the edges of
the beaten egg regularly so that the omelet
cooks evenly.
8. Gently tap the saucepan on the flame
until the contents are set, then remove the
omelet from the pot.
9. Position the skillet at a 45-degree
angle to the oven and shape the omelet.
10. To avoid browning, cook only until the
appropriate level of crispiness raises the
pan or decreases the steam. Transfer to a
warm plate and serve.

Baguette de France

Time to cook: 3 hours 10 minutes
Servings per container: 60

Ingredients:
10 oz. cold water
a little more flour
16 oz bread flour
2 tbsp. kosher salt
1 ½ teaspoons dried active yeast
1.75 oz. warm water

Method:
1. Weigh the hot water in a small cup and
sprinkle the fermentation on top.
2. Reintroduce the fermentation to allow it
to become liquid and disseminate.

3. Sift the wheat flour into a large mixing basin and whisk in the salt.
4. Make a well in the center of the butter mixture and stir in the absorbed yeast.
5. When cooking, add a few drops of cold water until the flour is stiff and hairy.
6. Cover the saucepan with cling film and set aside for thirty minutes.
7. Place the bread on a lightly oiled work surface and gently press it into a triangle, then cut it into thirds. Switch and loop at a 90-degree angle.
8. Place the dough in a large greased tub and cover with cling film.
9. Allowing it to grow will quadruple its volume in a warm place previously.
10. Divide the dough into four equal halves and shape each into a vertical-sided bread loaf.
11. Place the loaf on a lightly greased towel, cover it with greased cling film, and allow it to double in size.
12. Preheat the oven to 460°F and place it on a sheet pan with a water dish.
13. Remove the baguettes from the oven and place them on lightly oiled cookie sheets.
14. Using a lame, scissors, or razor blade, make four elongated slits, one away from the other.

15. Bake the loaf until it is crusty and moldy. When pressed, baguettes can produce a hollow sound.

Salad with Honeyed Fruit

Time to cook: 15 minutes
Size of each serving: 8

Ingredients:
¾ cup cherry
1 kiwifruit is optional.
2 peeled pears
2 pitted peaches
½ cup dry white wine
1 teaspoon sugar
1-pint hulled strawberries
2 tbsp lemon juice
½ teaspoon of zest
3 tablespoons honey

Method:
1. In a mixer, combine the ingredients and whip until the coating is creamy.
2. Relax for twenty seconds before serving.
3. Reduce or half the strawberries, slice the pears and berries into 34-inch sections and cut the fruit in half.
4. Cut the kiwifruit in half lengthwise and then cut each half lengthwise into 12-inch chunks.

5. Mix the ready fruit with the appropriate seasoning and serve immediately or cool.

Lorraine-style quiche

Time to cook: 55 minutes
Size of each serving: 8

Ingredients:
To make the pie crust
½ cup butter (125g)
1 big egg
½ teaspoon of salt
½ cup all-purpose flour (180g)

To be filled
½ cup Emmental cheese (150g)
seasoned with salt & pepper
½ cup milk (120 mL)
1/4 cup heavy cream (300 mL)
½ onion
1 cup bacon (200g)
4 huge eggs
1 tablespoon melted butter

Method:
1. In a large mixing bowl, combine the flour and a pinch of salt. Roll in the oil until you have a nice cookie-crumb consistency.

2. To ensure the materials adhere well, beat the eggs, form a solid dough, and chill for thirty minutes.
3. On a soft baking sheet, roll a wide wheel and row a 27 cm/8.6-inch spring arrangement.
4. Prick the pizza dough with a spoon and pre-bake it at 350F/180C for fifteen minutes.
5. Cook the onions in one tablespoon of oil over medium heat until they are tender, about eight minutes.
6. Fry the cut bacon in a deep fryer for about three minutes.
7. Whisk the egg whites, milk, and butter together.
8. Add the shredded Emmental cheese. Spray with salt and black pepper.
9. Arrange the fried onions in the pie crust and top with the cut bacon.
10. Spread the filling over it and bake for thirty minutes at 350°F (180°C) in the bottom area of the oven.
11. The pie is finished when it is perfect, and the filler has strengthened.
12. Caramelize with parmesan cheese. Serve immediately with the dessert.

Croissants with Almonds from France

Time to cook: 40 minutes

12 portion size

Ingredients:
To make the Almond Cream
½ cup almond flour
1 tbsp. all-purpose flour
a tsp vanilla extract
¼ tsp almond extract
granulated sugar ¼ cup
1 big egg
3 tablespoons softened butter

To complete
powdered sugar for dusting
½ cup almonds, sliced

Regarding the Croissants
17.25 oz puff pastry

To make the Egg Wash
1 tablespoon water
1 big egg

Method:
1. Preheat the oven to 400°F. Cover a
13x18-inch sheet pan with baking parchment.
2. Combine the sugar and butter in a medium
bowl. Mix everything together! Combine the
ingredients and the egg. Sprinkle again
when soft.

3. Add the almond flour and stir to combine. Add the all-purpose flour and blend until smooth again.

4. Combine the egg and one teaspoon of liquid in a small saucepan. Whisk quickly with a spoon until well combined. Simply set aside.

5. Using a pastry cutter or razor blade, cut the bread into three equal-sized rectangles.

6. Cut each rectangle into two long triangles.

7. Align the triangle so that both long edges face you.
Make a short incision at the long end of any triangle.

8. Squeeze two tablespoons of frangipane into each triangle.

9. Spread frangipane on each right triangular ground.

10. Add one teaspoon of dairy to the remaining frangipane and leave aside.

11. Spoon the mixture into croissants, starting at the long end and flattening the dough out a little at the wide end.

12. Repeat with the remaining pie crust layers, then place all of the croissants on the prepared baking sheet, 1 ½ inch apart.

13. Gently rub each croissant with the beaten egg, coating all bare parts.

14 Bake the mixture for fifteen minutes in a hot oven.

15. Scrub with the condensed frangipane from the furnace.

16. Remove the stove and replace it with a wire rack.

17. Allow the croissants to settle for ten minutes before sprinkling them with icing sugar.

Toast with French Radishes, Salt, and Butter

Time to cook: 5 minutes
Servings per recipe: 2

Ingredients:
The fleur de sel
Baguette toasted
1 pound European butter
French breakfast radishes, 1 bunch

Method:
1. Using a mandolin or a razor blade, cut the radishes into large, thin slices.
2. Arrange a sheet of cheese on top of each piece of bread, then top with radish slices and sprinkle with Fleur de Del.

Roll-up French Toast

Time to cook: 23 minutes
Size of each serving: 8

Ingredients:
3 teaspoons melted butter
The maple syrup
2 tablespoons ground cinnamon
8 nice white bread slices
¼ cup of milk
2 teaspoons sugar
3 tbsp unsweetened butter
1 tablespoon cinnamon powder
2 huge eggs
2 teaspoons brown sugar
3 teaspoons sugar

Method:
1. In a shallow oven cup, heat three
tablespoons of oil until it is just warm.
2. Using a spoon, combine two teaspoons of
icing sugar, two tablespoons of brown
sugar, and one tablespoon of spices to make
a creamy, spreadable mixture. Simply set
aside.
3. In a small bowl, combine the milk and
eggs. Just set it aside.
4. In a small bowl, combine two tablespoons
of granulated sugar and two tablespoons of
seasoning. Simply set aside.

5. After cutting each slice of bread's crust, stretch one loaf out to about 1/8-inch thick with a spoon.
6. Apply a thin layer of the flour mixture to each slice and tightly wrap.
7. Replace with the remaining flour mixture and bread slices.
8. Melt three tablespoons of melted butter in a large nonstick sauté pan over medium-high heat.
9. Dip one roll at a time into the beaten egg and set in the saucepan.
10. Allow the roll-ups to sauté for two minutes on each hand, or until lightly browned and somewhat crispy on the outside.
11. Place each roll on a work surface and lightly spray with the mixture.
12. Serve immediately with condensed milk.

Scrambled Eggs in French

Time to cook: 10 minutes
1 serving size

Ingredients:
1 tablespoon minced chives
2 toasted slices of country bread
3 huge eggs
3 tbsp whole milk
1 tbsp. unsalted butter

Method:

1. Begin by gently beating the egg whites in a small cup.
2. Heat the oil in a medium bowl over medium-high heat until gloopy.
3. Lightly whisk the eggs, then simmer and stir until set; gently fold in the dairy and chives.
4. Remove from the heat and serve with buttered toast.

2.2 Recipes for French Snacks and Sides

Snacks with Open-Faced Sausage

Time to cook: 10 minutes
 Serving size: 8

Ingredients:
1 minced garlic clove
48 cocktail rye bread slices
2 spring onions
1 tablespoon horseradish, prepared
1 pound pork sausage
1 cup shredded cheddar cheese
1 cup grated Parmesan cheese
1-quart mayonnaise

Method:

1. Preheat the oven to 375°F.
2. Combine all ingredients, except the bread, in a big cup.
3. Arrange toast slices in a thin layer on a cookie sheet.
4. Top with about a spoonful of sausage per person.
5. Bake for 10 minutes or until golden brown.

Snacks on Pizza Pinwheels

Time to cook: 32 minutes
Size of each serving: 8

Ingredients:
24 pepperoni slices
1 pizza sauce can
2 cups shredded mozzarella
1 roll of dough

Method:
1. Preheat oven to 375°F.
2. On a large baking sheet, shape the eight triangles of cone roll pastry into four rectangles.
3. Cover each rectangular with six slices of pepperoni or even quantities of fresh mozzarella.

4. Securely pull lengthwise and break into four or more portions together.
5. Bake until lightly browned in the oven, about 12 minutes.
6. Prepare with pizza sauce for frying.

Snack on Apples

1 hour of cooking time
Servings per recipe: 2

Ingredients:
½ teaspoon cinnamon powder
½ tsp coconut sugar
1 medium apple

Method:
1. Place the apple slices in a large Ziploc plastic bag and sprinkle with spices and chocolate powder.
2. Zip the container and spin it thoroughly to ensure all cuts are firmly covered.
3. Place it in a container refrigerated for at least an hour.
4. Store in a container for two days.

Snack for Unicorns

Time to cook: 25 minutes
Size of each serving: 16

Ingredients:
Candy pearls 1.75 ounces
1 tbsp. Unicorn Sprinkles
26 turquoise candy melts
26 candy melts in hot pink
26 candy melts violet
3 cups Bugles Original
1 cup candy melts (white)
1 cup pretzel rods
a quarter cup of cashew halves
1 ½ cup miniature marshmallows
1 cup Chex Rice Cereal

Method:
1. Scatter oats, pretzels, and peanuts on the baking sheets in a thin layer.
2. Place the lavender, bright pink, and turquoise candy melts in individual resealable plastic containers but do not close them.
3. Microwave it for 30 seconds on high.
4. Gently defrost with your fingertips, then heat in 30-second increments at 50% power until completely melted.
5. Wrap and snap the bag tips together.
6. Arrange the cereal, bagels, and peanuts in a baking dish.
7. Combine the bugles in a large mixing dish.
8. Melt white sweets in a small pan for 60 seconds at 50% capacity.

9. Combine thoroughly, then warm at 50% power in 20-second intervals until completely melted.
10. Apply the bugles and combine thoroughly to coat evenly.
11. Arrange on a casserole plate and sprinkle with sprinkles.
12. Cut the cereal, bagels, and cashew nuts into pieces.
13. Add the unicorn heads and seed solution.
14 Fold in the pancakes and serve in brightly colored paper cups.
15. Place any leftover food in an airtight container.

Power Snack with Peanut Butter

Time to cook: 10 minutes
12 bites per serving
Ingredients:
½ cup flax seeds, ground
2 teaspoons honey
½ cup chocolate chips, semi-sweet
1 cup oats, old fashioned
⅔ cup smooth peanut butter

Method:
1. Combine all five ingredients in a large mixing bowl. To blend, mix everything.

2. Chill them for thirty minutes to help to roll them easier.
3. Cut into 12 pieces and store in the refrigerator for up to a week.

Snack for Santa

Time to cook: 5 minutes
7-cup serving size

Ingredients:
½ cup chips peanut butter
½ cup white or vanilla chips
½ cup raisin
½ cup chocolate Christmas milk
2 chow Mein noodles
1 cup toasted honey-roasted peanuts
2 cups Cheerios Honey-Nut

Method:
1. Combine all of the ingredients in two broad-mouth quart cans.
2. Adorn it with string and silk.
3. Pour into a cup for eating and mix to combine.

Snack: Banana Cereal

Time to cook: 10 minutes
Servings per recipe: 3

Ingredients:
The peanut butter
1 cereal cup
2 ripe bananas

Method:
1. First, slice the bananas and divide them into sections.
2. Pour the grain onto the parchment paper, spread the butter over the banana, and add the grain to the peanut butter fruit.

Snack: Apple Sandwich

Time to cook: 5 minutes
1 serving size

Ingredients:
2 apple slices
2 granola tablespoons
½ teaspoon peanut butter

Method:
1. Spread whipped cream on half an apple slice; top with granola.
2. Place the remaining apple slice on top of the granola to finish the slice.

Snacks in the Shape of a Cornucopia

Time to cook: 15 minutes

12 portion size

Ingredients:
The glue gun
a dozen waffle cones
1 oz. honey cashews container
three yards of ribbon
1 pound cheddar crackers
1 cup cranberries with yogurt
1-pound pretzel crackers

Method:
1. Mix the parmesan potato chips, pretzel bagels, blueberries packed with yogurt, and cashew nuts in a mixing bowl. Simply set aside.
2. To make the cornucopia, pin the thread into 12 bows and stick the waffle poles together with a glue machine.
3. Fill each cornucopia with the cracker mixture.

Snack in a Pizza Cup

Time to cook: 40 minutes
Size of serving: 32 appetizers

Ingredients:
2 oz. pepperoni turkey
1 cup mozzarella cheese, shredded
¼ cup finely diced onion

¼ cup fresh green pepper
1 (8-ounce) can of pizza sauce
2 crescent roll tubes

Method:
1. Preheat the oven to 375°F.
2. Cut the dough pipes into eight rolls
each; cut the rounds in half.
3. Press dough into the bottom and sides of
tiny cupcake pans greased with oil.
4. Ladle pasta sauce into each cup.
5. Scatter the tomato, bell pepper,
pepperoni, and sausage.
6. Continue to cook until the slices are
golden brown and the cheese has melted.

Soup with French Onions

Time to cook: 80 minutes
Servings per recipe: 6

Ingredients:
8 French bread slices
1 ½ cups Swiss Gruyere
½ tsp black pepper
2 teaspoons brandy
2 bay leaves
1 tablespoon fresh thyme
6 medium red or yellow onions
8 cups beef broth
½ cup dry vermouth

4 tbsp olive oil
Salt
2 garlic cloves
1 tablespoon sugar
2 tbsp. melted butter

Method:
1. In a 5 to 6-quart thick saucepan over medium heat, warm three tablespoons of canola oil.
2. Add the vegetables and coat with the canola oil.
3. Cook the vegetables until soft, about 20 to 30 minutes, stirring often.
4. Raise the temperature to a comfortable level.
5. Add the remaining tablespoon of olive oil and the cheese and continue to cook for another fifteen minutes, stirring continuously, until the onions begin to tan.
6. Cook for another 5 to 10 minutes, until the veggies are thoroughly browned, then spray with sugars (to help with caramel flavors).
7. Add the chopped garlic and cook for another minute.
8. Transfer the vermouth to the pan's bottom edge and scrape up the golden-brown pieces, deglazing the bowl.

9. Season with additional salt and freshly ground black pepper to taste. Remove the bay leaves.
10. While the broth is bubbling, cover a baking sheet with parchment paper or foil and preheat the oven to 450 °F with a shelf in the top quarter of the oven.
11. Gently brush all sides of the French bread or croissant slices with olive oil.
12. Place it in the oven for about five minutes or until delicately golden brown. Remove from the oven and serve hot.

Salade Nicoise classique

Time to cook: 55 minutes
Size of each serving: 4

Ingredients:
2 5/12 oz. can Italian tuna
½ cup olives Nicoise
1 Boston lettuce head
6 radishes
¾ cup olive oil
1 tablespoon fresh thyme, chopped
pepper, freshly ground
8 little cherry tomatoes
12 shallots, chopped
2 teaspoons Dijon mustard
4 huge eggs
¼ cup vinegar (white wine)

1 pound russet potatoes
2 tablespoons white wine, dry
10 oz. haricots verts
Kosher salt is kosher salt.

Method:
1. Place the potatoes in a small saucepan,
cover with ice water, and season with salt.
2. Cooked until fork-tender, about five
minutes, then brought to a boil over medium
heat.
3. Drain and transfer to a small basin;
rain and chill with the champagne.
4. Bring a single marinated water casserole
dish to a boil.
5. In a pan, cover it with marinated cold
water.
6. Add the green beans to the boiling water
and cook for two to four minutes or until
crisp-tender and bright green.
7. Drain and immediately immerse in ice
cubes to cold; carefully rinse and dry.
8. Place the eggs in the selected saucepan
and cover with 1 inch of ice water.
9. Bring to a boil over medium heat, then
cover, turn off the heat, and set aside for
10 minutes.
10. Drain, then rush to the cool spray to
rest. Slice it with a chilly flowing spray.

11. Whisk the mustard, parsley, vinegar, tarragon, 12 teaspoon salt, and pepper in a cup.
Brush in the canola oil in a continuous, steady current until it is caramelized.
13. To compare, combine the tomato with salt and black pepper in a small pan.
14. Add ¼ cup of spice to the potatoes and turn. For a fifth, hard-boiled eggs.
15. Arrange peas, green beans, radishes, difficult eggs, and fish on top.
16. Add some vegetable fluids into the seasoning before adding the tomatoes to the dishes.

Salad Bistro Française

Time to cook: 20 minutes
Servings per recipe: 6

Ingredients:
¾ cup fresh parsley
½ cup toasted walnuts
½ cup fresh tarragon leaves
½ cup chopped chives
1 head of romaine lettuce
½ large head green oak
Eschalots Pickled in a Hurry
a third cup of red wine vinegar
4 teaspoons white sugar
2 eschalots

Dressing

5 teaspoons olive oil

½ tsp salt and pepper

1 teaspoon lemon juice

Method:

1. Add the vinegar and stir until the sugar dissolves.

2. Stir in eschalots, then set aside thirty minutes before it becomes fluffy or purple.

3. Shake the dressing in a pan.

4. Arrange a pile of lettuce on a plate.

5. Toss them gently with roughly a quarter of the coating.

6. Sprinkle on top of fresh spices, walnuts, and marinated eschalots.

7. Heavy rain and increased cloud cover. Immediately serve!

Chapter 3: Lunch and Dinner Main Courses

3.1 Main Courses for a French Lunch

Chicken Basque

Time to cook: 45 minutes
Size of each serving: 4

Ingredients:
100g ham de Bayonne

Season with salt and pepper to taste.
White wine, 100ml
1 pound fresh plum tomatoes
1.5 kg corn-fed whole chicken
1 tsp caster sugar
50ml of brandy
6 tbsp olive oil (extra virgin)
one bay leaf
4 thyme sprigs
3 shallots, banana
1 medium red pepper
1 medium green pepper
2 cloves garlic,

Method:
1. Preheat the oven to 200° C.
2. Cut two arms, two thighs, two breasts, and two chicken legs into eight pieces. Cut the breasts into two pieces.
3. Heat three tablespoons of oil in a pan, skillet, or casserole dish to cook the mixture.
4. Remove the ham from the grill and fry until crisp and clean on some paper towels.
5. Add the remaining garlic and bay leaf to the saucepan and wait until it jumps before adding the sliced shallots and pepper.
6. Cook for thirty minutes over medium heat, stirring occasionally, until the mixture is extremely smooth and finely caramelized.

7. Add the flambé and cognac, followed by the red wine.
8. After adding the fresh sliced tomatoes, cut the fluid in half.
9. Simmer the sauces for twenty minutes on medium heat or until the tomatoes are melted.
10. Season the sauce with salt and a tablespoon of icing sugar.
11. In a large skillet pan, heat the cooking oil and sear the fowl on both sides until lightly browned. Spray with salt and black pepper.
12. Place the chicken pieces in the boiling chili sauce, add the frying pan, and cook for 20 minutes.
13. Serve the Chicken Basquaise with a scattering of freshly cut parsley and fried Bayonne ham.

Chook au vin

1 hour 10 minutes to cook
Servings per recipe: 3

Ingredients:
½ pound onions, whole
Cremini mushrooms, ½ pound
2 tbsp unsweetened butter
1 ½ cups all-purpose flour
1 cup high-quality chicken stock

10 thyme sprigs, fresh
2 tbsp high-quality olive oil
14 oz. Cognac
½ bottle dry red wine
4 oz. quality bacon or pancetta
1 pound of chicken
1 sliced yellow onion
1 teaspoon garlic powder
Carrots, ½ pound
Kosher salt and freshly ground black pepper

Method:
1. Preheat oven to 250°F.
2. Heat the oil in a large roasting pan. Insert the bacon and bake for 10 to 15 minutes or until golden brown over medium-high heat.
3. Using a rubber spatula, transfer the bacon to a pan.
4. Meanwhile, spread the poultry flat on paper towels and press it dry. Spray the meat in both directions with pepper and salt.
5. Cook the chicken parts in a thin layer for about five minutes after the bacon is removed until they begin to color consistently.
6. Brown the chicken with the bacon from the dish until all of the chicken is done. Simply set aside.

7. Add the veggies, onion, two teaspoons of salt, and one teaspoon of peppers to the skillet and cook for 10 to 15 minutes, turning occasionally, over medium heat, until the vegetables are beautifully browned.
8. Remove the garlic and simmer for another two minutes.
9. Pour in the cognac and add the meat, poultry, and any liquids accumulated on the pan to the bowl.
10. Bring the juice, chicken broth, and tarragon to a boil.
11. Cover the basin with a tight-fitting lid and bake for thirty minutes or until the chicken is yellow.
12. Remove it from the oven and place it on the grill.
13. Puree one tablespoon of the oil and the starch and stir into the sauce.
14. Stir in the preserved onions. In a big marinade pan, heat the remaining one tablespoon of oil and fry the mushroom for ten minutes or until brown and crispy. Pour into the broth.
15. Bring the stew to a boil, then cook for another ten minutes. Season before serving. Serve it hot.

Spring Vegetable Barigoule

1 hour 10 minutes to cook
Servings per recipe: 6

Ingredients:
For garnish, use cilantro sprigs.
Sea salt flake from Maldon
Kosher salt is kosher salt.
1 tsp vanilla bean
3 tbsp. sherry vinegar
ground black pepper, freshly ground
5 black peppercorns, whole
1 bay leaf
Snow peas, 4 oz.
⅓ cup peas, fresh
4 cup vegetable broth
10 thyme sprigs
4 baby fennel bulbs
4 spring onion bulbs
6 small carrots
¼ cup extra virgin olive oil
10 garlic cloves
½ tsp coriander seeds
1 pencil asparagus bunch

Method:
1. Bring a 6-quart steamed water casserole
dish to a boil.
2. In batches, process snow peas, lentils,
vegetables, and asparagus until buttery,
about two minutes for peas and three
minutes for veggies and asparagus.

3. Place the vegetables in an ice bath to cool; rinse, discard the asparagus rubber band, and put aside.
4. Clean over medium heat for two minutes, then pan dry and toast coriander powder.
5. Add 14 cup oil; roast garlic until crispy, 3-4 minutes, then transfer to a cup with a rubber spatula.
6. Cook celery and white onions until crispy, about ten minutes; mix in a dish with cloves.
7. Add the sliced onion leaves, reserve, tarragon, bay leaves, black pepper, and vanilla bean; simmer for about thirty minutes or until significantly reduced.
8. Strain the product and return it to the skillet; whisk in the vinegar, black pepper, and remaining water and continue to cook.
9. Stir in all vegetables; sauté, wrap, and cook for four minutes or until the vegetables are tender.
10. Arrange vegetables on top of bowls and top with broth; season with coriander sprigs and kosher salt.
Paillarded chicken

Time to cook: 34 minutes
Size of each serving: 4

Ingredients:

4 (6 oz.) chicken breasts
Salad
4 cups arugula, trimmed
8 oz. cherry tomatoes
1 lemon, freshly squeezed
½ teaspoon black pepper
½ teaspoon of salt
1 tbsp olive oil (extra virgin)
2 tbsp. lemon zest
1 tbsp. red wine vinegar
Marinade
2 tsp extra virgin olive oil
1 smashed garlic clove
1 lemon, freshly squeezed
1 chopped small shallot
⅓ cup white wine, dry

Method:
1. Using a wooden skewer or a hard skillet, press chicken breasts to 14 thickness on a work surface.
2. Combine the liquor, one lime juice, shallots, two teaspoons of oil, and garlic in a small dish. Allow the chicken thighs to marinate for fifteen minutes.
3. In a large mixing bowl, combine two lime juices, syrup, two tablespoons of olive oil, and lime zest; stir in 14 teaspoons of salts and powder.
4. Toss in the tomatoes and butternut squash.

5. Preheat a high-heat outdoor grill, lightly oil the fryer, or heat a skillet over medium heat.
6. Remove the chicken from the marinade and sprinkle with the remaining 14 teaspoon salt.
7. Cook the chicken on a wire rack grill until lightly browned and completely cooked, two to three minutes on each side.
8. A temperature gauge with a center insert that can read at least 175 degrees F.
9. Arrange the chicken over the arugula bowl.

Apple Cinnamon Bostock

1 hour and 25 minutes of cooking time
Servings per recipe: 6

Ingredients:
To make the Frangipane
1 teaspoon vanilla essence, pure
1 tsp. Calvados
1 pound unsalted butte
½ tsp kosher salt
1 cup almonds, sliced
2 huge eggs
¼ cup granulated sugar
Regarding the Toasts
1 ⅓ cup almonds, sliced
granulated sugar

¼ cup cinnamon syrup, prepared
¼ cup apple sauce
6 pieces milk bread 6 slices white bread
Spray with nonstick cooking spray

Method:
1. Combine 1 cup almonds and sugar in a mixing dish and finely chop. Eggs, sugar, and salt are blended into a fine powder.
2. Transfer the mixture to a jar and set aside to cool for thirty minutes or until midnight. Drizzle with vanilla and Calvados, stirring to combine.
3. Place a shelf in the center of the oven and preheat to 375°.
4. Line a broadsheet pan with parchment paper and lightly oil the paper with a clean towel.
5. Place the bread on a baking sheet and liberally coat both sides with the cinnamon sauce.
6. Spread one tablespoon of apple sauce and ¼ cup almond paste on one half of each slice.
7. Place the remaining 11 cups of sliced almonds in a shallow basin.
Push the ready toast into the nut bowl to cover the frangipane layer with nuts.
9. Place the bread on a baking sheet, almond side up.

10. Cook for 20 minutes, or until the
almonds are toasted, and the frangipane is
puffy and firm but still tender.
11. Scrub with icing sugar and serve hot or
at room temperature.

Marinières Moules

1 hour of cooking time
Size of each serving: 4

Ingredients:
Salt
Pepper
4 mussels
1 tablespoon of flour
Parsley
2 shallots
⅛ teaspoon dry white wine
30 g margarine or butter

Method:
1. Finely chop the shallots.
2. Thoroughly scratch and clean the
mussels.
3. Place them in a casserole dish with
butter, shallots, and balsamic vinegar.
4. In the lidded casserole bowl, cover them
for several minutes over medium heat. Blend
2-3 times while cooking.

5. Remove the mussels from the soup pot while still open, retaining the frying liquids. Please keep them warm in a single deep dish.
6. Return the juice to the flame.
7. Combine 1 teaspoon of starch, 1 spoon, and the same quantity of margarine.
8. Combine everything from the mussels boiling on the flame. Allow it to simmer for a few minutes.
9. Arrange the mussels on top. Spray with cooking spray and top with grated parmesan.

Fish in Basque Style with Green Peppers and Manila Clams

Time to cook: 25 minutes
Size of each serving: 4

Ingredients:
12 clams from Manila
1 tsp pimento d'Espelette
2 teaspoons parsley
2 pounds boneless hake
1 pound mild green pepper
1 large Spanish onion
1 cup olive oil (extra virgin)
2 cups fish broth
a quarter teaspoon kosher salt
2 garlic cloves
¼ cup white wine, dry

1 tbsp. all-purpose flour

Method:
1. Melt the butter in a 12-inch skillet over medium to low heat.
2. Add the garlic and heat for 1 minute, stirring frequently, until lightly browned.
3. Scatter the starch over the cloves and whisk to combine.
4. Add the wine and simmer for about two minutes or until slightly thickened and reduced.
5. Return the water to a boil after adding the fish stock and sea salt.
6. Arrange the tomatoes, onions, and tarragon on the bottom border uniformly.
7. Reduce the heat to medium, place the bowl in the pan, and cook for about five minutes or until the vegetables are soft.
8. Open the bowl and place the skin of the fish portions on top of the vegetables in a clear layer.
9. Dip the clams and season the seafood to fit between the cutlets.
10. Cook for seven minutes until the middle of the fillets is slightly transparent and the clams are free.
11. Arrange the vegetables on a large baking sheet, followed by the tuna and clams.

12. Drizzle the remaining liquid over the salmon and, if using, top with grated parmesan and Espelette paprika; serve immediately.

Diane's Steak

Time to cook: 30 minutes
Servings per recipe: 2

Ingredients:
1 teaspoon fresh parsley
Spicy sauce
1 tsp Worcestershire sauce
1 tablespoon chopped scallions
¼ cup of heavy cream
¼ cup demi-glace veal
¼ oz. Cognac
1 garlic bulb
¼ pounds of button mushrooms
Kosher salt with black pepper
1 shallot, small
½ teaspoon olive oil
4 ounces beef tenderloin
1 tbsp. unsalted butter
2 teaspoons Dijon mustard

Method:
1. Heat the oil in a big skillet.

2. Season the meat with pepper and salt and cook until the edges are slightly golden brown, about 1 minute, over medium heat.
3. Bake the medallions for 45 seconds more, then transfer to a foil sheet and cover.
4. Add the tarragon and cloves to the pan and cook over medium heat, swirling once aromatic, for about 20 seconds.
5. Add the mushroom, season with salt, and cook for approximately two minutes or until melted.
6. Remove the fuse from the flame, insert the Cognac, and carefully light it.
7. After the smells have died down, add the vinegar and yogurt and stir for two minutes over low heat.
8. Combine the Worcestershire sauce, green onions, and tarragon in the veal demi-glace and season with salt, pepper, and hot sauce to taste.
9. Add the steak and any remaining juices to the frying pan and turn to coat.
10. Boil for 1 minute or until well warmed. Transfer the beef to the pans, top with the sauces, and serve.

3.2 Main Courses for a French Dinner

Suzette's Crepes

Time to cook: 45 minutes
Size of each serving: 8

Ingredients:
To make the crêpes
¼ teaspoon of salt
1 tablespoon melted butter
2 tbsp. orange juice
½ teaspoon orange rind
2 eggs
2 tbsp. melted butter
1 cup regular flour
½ cup minus 1 tablespoon water
½ cup of milk

To make the Orange Syrup
4 tbsp. granulated sugar
4 oz. Grand Marnier
16 teaspoons melted butter
Vanilla ice cream as a garnish

Method:
1. Gather your ingredients.
2. Mix the milk, flour, orange zest, two tablespoons of butter, orange juice, water, eggs, and salts until completely smooth; chill the mixture for twenty minutes before making the crêpes.

3. Combine the rice, butter, eggs, buttermilk, fruit juice, orange zest, and spice for the Crepes Suzette method.
4. Melt one teaspoon of butter in a crêpe tray or wide pan over low heat.
5. Stir in three teaspoons of flour until the bottom of the container is covered in batter.
6. Cook for ten minutes or until the crêpe is slightly soft on top and crispy underneath.
7. Slide the spoon underneath it, remove the sides of the crêpe, and gently turn it upside-down into the basin. Heat for two minutes, then transfer the fried crêpe to a pan to keep warm.
Repeat the procedure with the remaining mixture. Simply set aside.
8. In a medium saucepan set over medium-high heat, heat a portion of the oil until it fizzes.
9. Sprinkle half the sugar over the melting fat and remove the pan from the heat.
10. Pour in half of the Grand Marnier, being careful not to burn the pan.
11. Transfer the crêpes to the tray and brush all sides with the citrus syrup.
Roll or fold the crêpes into quarters to make pipes.
13. To make more citrus syrup, heat the residual butter in the pan, remove it from

the heat, and add the sweet syrup and Grand
Marnier.
14. Place a bowl of ice cream beside each
crepe and drizzle the citrus syrup over the
Suzette crepe.

Rillettes de saumons
1 hour 45 minutes to cook
2 cups serving size

Ingredients:
¼ teaspoon paprika dulce
Baguette toasted
½ teaspoons lemon juice
1 tbsp olive oil (extra virgin)
¼ pound smoked salmon
1 shallot, big
4 cups water
1 teaspoon ground black pepper
1 cup white wine, dry
5 teaspoons unsalted butter
1 medium onion
1 bay leaf
½ tbsp. sour cream
1 rib celery
1 leek, cut in half lengthwise
Salt
ground white pepper, freshly ground
2 tbsp. chives, snipped
1 liqueur tablespoon
½ pound fillet salmon

Method:

1. Spray both the fish on a tray with anise liqueur and season with salt and red pepper.

2. Cover with cling film and set aside for thirty minutes at room temperature.

3. Meanwhile, in a medium pan, bring the celery, parsnip, cabbage, bay leaves, coriander seeds, vinegar, and liquid to a boil. Simmer for 25 minutes.

4. Place the fish in the pot, cover it, and set it aside for ten minutes.

5. Cover the fish, remove the bay leaves, and place it in the fridge for 45 minutes to cool. Make some fish flakes.

6. In a pan, crumble one tablespoon of the oil. Over medium heat, add the red onion and cook until tender. Allow it to cool.

7. Meanwhile, in a small bowl, cream together the remaining four tablespoons of melted butter. Blend in the crème fraiche.

8. Add the chilled shallot, dill, lime juice, canola oil, and parmesan to the pickled and roasted fish and mix until combined.

9. Seasoning and sea salt can be used to flavor rillettes. Serve with toasted baguette slices.

The Perfect Pot Roast

3 hours 45 minutes to cook
Size of each serving: 8

Ingredients:
1 baguette de France
1 pound of gruyere cheese
2 tbsp. Worcestershire sauce
6 fresh thyme sprigs
chuck roast (3-4 pounds)
four yellow onions
4 cups beef stock
1 tsp. kosher salt
¼ tsp black pepper
2 tbsp of vegetable oil

Method:
1. Preheat the oven to 325°F.
2. The sea salt, spice, and tarragon flavor the chuck roast.
3. Place the olive oil in a basin and heat it.
4. Add the chuck and brown it for five minutes on each side until it swirls and is heavy.
5. Add the carrots, Worcestershire sauce, livestock broth, and tarragon and cook, covered, for 3 to 312 hours.
6. Remove the leaves from the oven and cover with foil.
7. Preheat the oven to high broil.

8. Cut the meat into large bits.
9. Serve with sliced baguettes and Gruyere cheese.
10. Place the bowl in the oven for 1-2 minutes, exposed, until the cheese begins to melt and smoke.
11. Serve immediately.

Salad with Lentils and Pork

Cooking Time: 40 minutes
6 servings

Ingredients:
1 red onion
Kosher salt and freshly ground black pepper
3 tbsp white wine vinegar
3 tbsp parsley
1 rib celery
3 tbsp Dijon mustard
1 tiny yellow onion
1 pound skinless pork belly
2 carrots
1 pound of lentils
6 whole cloves

Method:
1. Pierce the garlic with the onions.
2. In a large frying pan, combine the onions, vegetables, pulled pork, carrot,

and fennel with 6 cups of water. Bring it to a boil.
3. To keep the lentils tender, keep the heat low and cover for 15 minutes.
4. Thinly slice the celery and vegetables, then cut the pork into 14-inch pieces.
5. Combine the vinegar and mustard in a large mixing bowl.
6. Add the lentils, parsley, spring onion, sugar, and peppers to the vegetables, cover, and set aside. To serve, transfer to a cup.

Pork Roast with Honey Glazed Apples

Time to cook: 2 hours and 30 minutes
Size of each serving: 4

Ingredients:
2 cups of dry apple cider
5 sweet-tart apples, whole
a pound of unsalted butter
2 large yellow onions
1 or 2 pork roasts
4 thyme sprigs
4 sprigs rosemary
2 teaspoon honey
Kosher salt and freshly ground black pepper

Method:

1. Preheat the oven to 350°F. Place the meat in a large casserole dish and season with salt.
2. Sprinkle the sugar over the meat, then sprinkle with the thyme.
3. Pour the oil over the pork, then add the onion from around the pig flesh to the bowl.
4. Pour the vinegar into the skillet and roast for 45 minutes, or until the temperature gauge in the center of the meat registers 120°.
5. Remove the apples from the meat and bake for another forty minutes, or until the apples are tender and the meat is beautifully browned, and the temperature gauge reads 160°.
6. Remove the pan from the oven and set aside for 20 minutes.
7. Transfer the meat to a big platter and chop it into tiny slices.
8. To serve, scatter the fried onions and apples around the meat and drizzle with the cooking liquid.

Squid Provençal Stuffed

1 hour of cooking time
Size of each serving: 4

Ingredients:

For garnish, use wild arugula leaves.
For serving, lemon wedges
1 ½ pound cleaned medium squid
1-quart white wine
Chipotle pepper
2 tsp. lemon zest
chard or spinach, 12 oz.
4 oiled anchovy fillets
4 cloves garlic
Kosher salt is kosher salt.
2 teaspoon thyme, chopped
½ teaspoon rosemary, chopped
5 teaspoons olive oil
ground black pepper, freshly ground
3 teaspoons parsley
1 medium onion
¼ cup dry bread crumbs

Method:
1. Caramelize the chard in hot boiling
water for two minutes, then rinse and chill
under running water.
2. Squeeze the chard until completely dry
before cutting it thinly. Simply set aside.
3. Melt the remaining tablespoon of coconut
oil in a small skillet over medium-high
heat.
4. Add the toast crumbs and cook for two or
three minutes, flipping frequently, until
golden brown and buttered.

5. Remove the skillet from the heat and set aside to cool the bread crumbs.

6. Heat three tablespoons of canola oil in a pan over medium-high heat.

7. Place the onions in the pan, season with salt, and roast for about ten minutes or until finely browned and melted.

8. Combine the garlic, tarragon, thyme, smoked paprika, anchovies, and cloves in a mixing bowl.

9. Cook for another two minutes, stirring occasionally. Place the onion mixture on a plate.

10. Stir in the sauteed chard, conserved bread scraps, and lime juice. Blend thoroughly with a rolling pin. Change your spice taste.

11. Thoroughly rinse the squid and wipe it down with icy water.

12. Use a teaspoon to fill each squid's body, being careful not to overfill it.

13. Use a toothpick to secure the lower section. Season the stuffed squid with salt and black pepper using both hands.

14. Season the tentacles separately with pepper and salt.

15. Heat and fry a cast-iron pan for 5 minutes over medium heat.

16. Pour in 1 tablespoon olive oil, add the squid, and roast for 4 minutes, flipping once, until beautifully browned.

17. Apply the wine by inserting tentacles from surrounding limbs.
18. Cover and simmer for about two minutes, or until the squid heads and tentacles are soft but solid.
19. Remove the lid and heat for another two minutes, or until the wine has somewhat decreased. Season with salt and pepper.
20. Transfer the squid bodies and tentacles to a large baking tray.
21. Arrange the butternut squash around the squid and serve with shredded cheese.

Mussels with a Herb Vinaigrette

Time to cook: 35 minutes
Servings per recipe: 6

Ingredients:
Kosher salt is kosher salt.
Espelette pimento
½ preserved lemon rind
1 lime juice
2 flat-leaf parsley sprigs
2 tarragon sprigs
2 c. olive oil
4 chives, entire
6 ½ pound mussels, cleaned
½ cup white wine, dry
2 tbsp. vegetable oil
2 minced garlic cloves

6 minced whole shallots

Method:
1. In a frying pan over medium-high heat, steam the duck fat.
2. Add the parsley and cloves and cook for about 5 minutes or until melted but not golden brown.
3. Raise the heat to medium-high, then add the liquor and mussels and cover them.
4. Cook for 5 minutes, shifting the pan slightly as the mussels swell. Get rid of those that don't open.
5. Transfer the mussels to a work surface using tongs or a spatula.
6. Drain the boiling liquid through a sieve in a shallow saucepan and scrape the parsley and cloves into a big dish.
7. Bring the remaining liquid to a boil and simmer for around fifteen minutes before reducing to ¾ cup.
8. Remove the plate from the fire and let it cool completely.
9. Pour ¼ cup of the reduced liquid into the spring onions and cloves, then add the canola oil, dill, tarragon, estragon, lime juice, and lemon zest.
10. Toss until well combined. Dress with salts and Espelette pigment.

11. Remove and discard the hollow top cones from each mussel, and transfer the bottoms to a big platter.
12. Drizzle the vinaigrette over the mussels and serve over rice.

Chicken Lyon-Style with Vinegar Sauce

1 hour of cooking time
Size of each serving: 4

Ingredients:
¼ c. crème fraîche
Steamed Rice with Herbs
1 cup vinegar de Banyuls
2 cup chicken broth
12 garlic cloves, big
1 bay leaf
3 tbsp olive oil
seasoned with salt & pepper
3 tbsp. unsalted butter
1 pound of chicken

Method:
1. Preheat the oven to 450°F. In a large, dark pan, heat the oil.
2. Season the fowl with salt and black pepper, transfer to a skillet, and cook until golden brown over medium-high heat.
3. Add three tablespoons of oil to the pan and toss to coat the meat.

4. Replace the chicken skin sides and top
with the cloves and green leaves.
5. Place the pan in the oven for ten
minutes or until all of the chicken chunks
are just clean. Place the breast portions
on a tray.
6. Return the pan to the oven and roast the
leftover chicken for another fifteen
minutes, frying it for a few minutes before
it is cooked.
7. Add the meat and cloves to the pan.
8. Pour in the chicken stock and reduce to
14 cups, about ten minutes. Carefully
remove the golden brown bits.
9. Stir in the crème fraiche and the
remaining two teaspoons of oil.
10. Return the meat to the pan, along with
any remaining liquids.
11. Cook, frequently basting, over medium-
high heat until the sauce is mildly
thickened and the chicken is cooked through
about three minutes.
12. Season with salt and pepper to taste
and serve over boiling herbed beans.

Roasted Veal Blanquette

2 hours 30 minutes to cook
Size of each serving: 8

Ingredients:

1 pound green peas
2 egg yolks
½ pounds of mushrooms
2 tbsp. all-purpose flour
1 pound russet potatoes
½ pounds of white onions
¼ tsp dried thyme
4 halved carrots
4 pounds roast veal shoulder

Method:
1. In an 8-quart Dutch oven, dark roast all surfaces over medium heat.
2. Combine the tarragon and two cups of water. Reduce the heat to medium and simmer for thirty minutes.
3. Add the carrots, onions, and potatoes to the mixing bowl.
4. Cook for thirty minutes, covered. Toss the spores in. Wrap and cook for 30 minutes or until the vegetables and veal are tender.
5. Remove the vegetables from the oven and keep them warm.
6. In a mixing basin, blend the flour and two tablespoons of water until smooth. In the Dutch oven, constantly stir the mixture.
7. In a small cup, whisk together the egg yolks. In small amounts, add any spicy gravy.

8. Slowly pour the egg yolk mixture into the gravy and whisk until it thickens. The rest of the gravy should be served.

Bourguignon de Boeuf

Time to cook: 3 hours 15 minutes
Servings per recipe: 6

Ingredients:
1 pound shiitake mushrooms
2 tbsp. melted butter
2 tbsp chopped fresh parsley
two bay leaves
1 crushed beef bouillon cube
2-3 cups beef broth
12 pearl onions, tiny
3 quarts red wine
2 tbsp tomato paste
1 tsp salt and pepper
2 teaspoons flour
1 tsp. fresh thyme
1 big sliced white onion
6 minced garlic cloves
1 tablespoon extra virgin olive oil
3-pound brisket of beef
1 medium carrot
bacon (6 ounces)

Method:

1. In a broad saucepan or pan, sauté the beef in 1 tablespoon of oil for about three minutes, or until crispy and golden.
2. Transfer to a six-quart (liter) stir-fry dish.
3. Wrap dry meat in a clean cloth and cook in batches until both oil sides are golden brown.
4. Add the veggies and tomatoes to the stir-fry pan with the pork.
5. To finish, stir in ½ teaspoon fine salt and ¼ teaspoon ground black pepper.
6. Pour the wine into the pan or skillet and allow it to simmer for five minutes before stirring in the starch.
7. Reduce and sweeten it significantly, then combine it with two cups of stock, tomato sauce, cloves, bullion, and spices in the crockpot.
8. Mix all of the ingredients thoroughly.
9. Cook for six hours on high heat or eight hours on medium heat or until the meat is split and tender.
10. In the last five minutes of the slow cooker, begin prepping the mushrooms by warming the butter in a medium skillet over medium-high heat.
11. Add the remaining two garlic cloves and cook until the garlic is aromatic (about 30 seconds), then transfer the mushrooms.

12. Cook for about five minutes, moving the pot halfway through to brush with the sugar. Season with salt if desired.
13. Before serving, stir the meat stew and combine it with the liquid.
14. Garnish with fresh parsley and serve with potato salad, rice, or pasta.

Recipe for Flamiche

1 hour 50 minutes to cook
Size of each serving: 8

Ingredients:
Regarding the Crust
ten tbsp. unsalted butter
4 tbsp of ice water
½ teaspoon of salt
1 ¼ cup flour
Filling with leeks and bacon
two big, lightly beaten eggs
1 ½ cup Gruyere cheese, shredded
a third of a cup whole milk
a sprinkle of nutmeg, grated
2 teaspoons flour
a third of a cup of white wine
Season with salt and pepper to taste.
¼ cup cream fraiche
1 big chopped shallot
5 big leeks
3 teaspoons melted butter

5 ounces diced bacon

Method:
1. Combine the flour and baking powder in a large mixing bowl.
2. Using a pastry knife, cut the diced oil and butter into the powder until the consistency is a coarse powder.
3. Add one tablespoon of flour and mix until the dough comes together, adding water as needed.
4. Carefully transfer the mixture to a 10-inch tart pan and cool for thirty minutes or until solid.
5. Preheat the oven to 425 degrees Fahrenheit.
6. Use a spoon to pierce the crust's edge.
7. Cut a square of parchment paper about four inches smaller than the pie plate.
8. Place the sheet on the bottom and fill it with ceramic pie pounds.
9. Bake for 10 minutes in the oven or until it is done.
10. Remove the paper and scales from the stove and allow them to cool.
11. Bake the sliced bacon in a large oven over medium heat for about five minutes or until crispy and lightly browned.
12 Remove the bacon from the plate using a rubber spatula.

13 Remove all except one teaspoon of the bacon fat.

14. Add the oil and the shallot slices until melted.

Heat for about two minutes or until the mixture is translucent.

15. Add the sliced leeks and mix to coat with the oil.

16. Pour in the red wine, partially cover, and cook until the chives are soft, about ten minutes, stirring occasionally. Spice with pepper, salt, and nutmeg.

17. Replace the bacon in the pan. Stir in the flour and cook for a minute or two, stirring constantly.

18. Stir in the milk until the mixture thickens.

Incorporate the crème fraiche into the mixture.

19. Allow it to cool before removing it from the heat.

20. Next, whisk the eggs and 1 cup of Gruyere cheese.

21. Pour the filling solution into the designated crust to assemble the pie.

Spread the remaining cheese evenly over the top.

22. Toast for 30 minutes or until cooked and thoroughly browned.

Allow it to settle for at least a few minutes before serving.

24. Serve warm or at room temperature.

Confit de Canard

Time to cook: 20 minutes
4 duck legs per person

Ingredients:
2 tablespoons black peppercorns
2 to 4 cups duck fat, rendered
1/2 sprigs parsley
10 fresh thyme sprigs
1 medium onion
6 medium garlic cloves
four duck legs
6 shallots, big
1 teaspoon salt

Method:
1. Season both sides of the duck legs with salt and pepper; set aside.
2. In a spice grinder bowl, combine the parsley, onions, cloves, and tarragon and pulse until finely diced but not puréed, about fifteen pulses.
3. Transfer half of the vegetable solution to a non-reactive pan, such as a casserole tray, that can fit duck limbs securely and evenly.
4. Scatter half of the sage leaves and coriander seeds over the vegetable mixture,

then insert the skin-side duck legs into the vegetable mixture with an equal top layer.

5. Spread the remaining mint leaves and coriander seeds, together with the veggie mixture, evenly over the duck legs, so that they are entirely covered.

6. Put duck feet, vegetable blend, rosemary, and coriander seeds in a one-gallon zipper-lock bag.

7. When you're ready to cook, move the stovetop to the middle position and preheat the oven to 105°C.

8. Melt the duck fat in a toaster pan or 3-quart reduced saucer.

9. eliminate the duck feet from the solution and clean out as much of the solution paste as possible before rinsing the limbs under cold water to eliminate any additives; discard the solution.

10. Clean the duck feet with cloths, then place them in a thin layer in a duck fat saucer (if using) to ensure they are completely saturated in oil.

11. Alternatively, tightly pack the duck limbs in a shallow baking dish and coat them with melted duck fat to ensure that the legs are entirely covered in fat.

12. Place the tray or serving dish in the oven and cover it with a cover or sheet of metal.

13. Cook until the duck is entirely soft
and, when poked with a serrated knife, the
meat shows almost no discomfort and the
meat has begun to peel away from the lower
of the drumstick, 3 12 to 4 hours.
14. Remove the duck from the boiling vessel
and chill it to room temperature, and
immerse it in fat.

Chapter 4: French Desserts and Bread Recipes

4.1 Dessert Recipes

Crème Brulee

Cooking Time: 4 hours and 50 minutes
8 servings

Ingredients:
¼ teaspoon salt
1 ½ teaspoon vanilla extract
3 cups heavy cream
½ teaspoon espresso powder
¾ cup granulated sugar
5 big egg yolks

Method:
1. Preheat the oven to 163°C.
2. Combine all the yolks and half a cup of the sugar syrup. Just set it aside.
3. Combine the cream cheese, coffee powder, and salts in a small saucepan over medium heat.
4. Remove from the heat as soon as it begins to boil. Incorporate the vanilla powder.

5. Pour roughly half a cup of warm crème Fraiche and whisk the egg yolks steadily.
6. Keep shifting the egg yolks so they don't scatter.
7. Press and stir the egg yolk solution in a moderate yet steady stream.
8. Arrange the ramekins on a large baking tray.
9. If you don't have a large enough pan, fry them in separate bowls.
10. Divide the custard evenly among the ramekins.
11. Carefully cover the pan with about half an inch of heated water.
12. Use an oven mitt gently o transfer the baking tray to the oven; the baking platter will be hot.
13. Bake until the sides and cores are firm and spongy.
14. The amount of time depends on the size of your ramekin.
15. They are finished when an immediate read thermometer reads 170 °F for a more exact symbol.
16. Place it on a chopping board for at least 1 hour to settle.
17. Refrigerate for at least three hours and up to two days before finishing.
18. Sprinkle the remaining granulated sugar over the top of the cooled custard.

19. Use a heat torch to crisp up the sweets and consume them immediately, or place it in the fridge for up to 2 hours before eating.

Cookies Palmier

1 hour of cooking time
Size of each serving: 4

Ingredients:
4 tbsp melted butter
1 cup pure cane sugar
1 frozen sheet puff pastry

Method:
1. Unwrap the puff pastry.
2. Once you have your puff crust, flatten the sides with your palms or a wooden spoon to get an even rectangular shape.
3. Brush evenly melted butter over the puff dough.
4. Spray a quarter of the sugar onto the crust and evenly divide it around this one.
5. Using a spoon, roll the dough into a large oval, pushing the sugar into the dough.
6. Turn the pastry and repeat the cycle, rubbing with the remaining butter and sugar.

7. Roll the pastry foundation firmly into the end, starting in the middle, then moving the tops of the sheet to reach the center as well.
8. The rolled scale will be the same. Wrap with cling film for about thirty minutes and relax.
9. Preheat the oven to 220 degrees Celsius. Line a cookie dish with a paper towel.
10. Remove the protective wrap and place one of the wraps on top of the other.
11. Shave the irregular sides of the pastry, then cut into ½ inch (1 cm) pieces. They have to look like smashed-up hearts.
12. Arrange the strips on the baking tray about 2 inches (5 cm) apart to allow for mobility.
13. Bake for 15 minutes, or until the sugar is well browned, and the sweets are pale yellow, turning halfway through.

Financiers

Time to cook: 50 minutes
Size of Servings: 24

Ingredients:
½ tsp vanilla extract
2 ½ oz. Brown butter
a generous teaspoon of salt
4 egg whites, big

2 teaspoons sugar
5 teaspoons flour
1 cup hazelnut or almond flour

Method:
1. Preheat the oven to 375°F and carefully butter the insides of 24 small puffs of pastries with warmed, not molten, butter, making sure to coat the higher rims of the creases.
2. In a medium-sized dish, combine the almond or hazelnut combination, salt, and flour mixture.
3. Add the egg whites and extract, then the sugar caramelizes.
4. Cut each small puff pastry incision almost to the tip.
5. To level the tips, firmly tap the tins on the counter, then bake for ten minutes or until golden brown.
6. Allow the financiers to heat them in the cartons, cut them, and use a paring blade to help liberate them if feasible.

Galette with Apples and Cranberries

Time to cook: 45 minutes
12 portion size

Ingredients:
In the Pastry

6 tbsp soured cream
½ cup iced water
¼ teaspoon of salt
½ tbsp. unsalted butter
6 tbsp white cornmeal
1 tsp of sugar
1-quart all-purpose flour

In order to Fill
1 ½ cup cranberries, fresh
2 tbsp. unsalted butter
½ teaspoon cinnamon powder
8 medium apples
½ cup granulated sugar
3 teaspoon honey
3 tbsp freshly squeezed lemon juice
½ cup of water

Method:
1. In a mixing basin, combine the rice, cornstarch, salt, and sugar to make the pastry.
2. Spread the fat cubes over the edge and rotate for a few seconds or until the fat parts are the size of peanut peas.
3. In a small pan, combine the cream fraiche and crushed ice.
4. Sprinkle and pulse the paste over the flour until it is soft and cohesive.
5. Form the dough into a ball, wrap it in plastic wrap, and chill for 20 minutes.

6. In the meantime, make the sauce by combining the syrup, water, butter, lime juice, and spices in a large skillet over medium heat and baking, swirling, until the sugar is dissolved.

7. Stir in the sliced apples and cook for about five minutes or until the apples soften.

8. Transfer the apple slices to a cup using a rubber spatula.

9. Add the walnuts to the fluid in the frying pan and heat for about two minutes or until they begin to rise.

10. Transfer the cranberries to the container with the apple using a rubber spatula.

11. Reduce the heat to medium and simmer the water, then spoon over the fruits until much reduced.

12. Place two racks in the center of the oven and preheat to 400°F.

13. Cut the dough in half. Pull each quarter out into a 12-inch-long round shape on a lightly floured surface and transfer to separate baking sheets.

14. Divide the fruit filling evenly between the pastry rounds and place it in a uniform layer, leaving a 12-inch border exposed.

15. Place the border over the berries.

16. The fat strips are placed over the exposed fruit.

17. Sprinkle sugar on the cookie rims.
18. Cook the galettes, turning them 180 degrees halfway through, until the pie is gently browned and the apples are tender 40 to 45 minutes.
19. Transfer the pans to a wire rack and allow the galettes to cool completely. Consume with crème fraîche.

Tarte aux figs de France

1 hour 10 minutes to cook
Size of each serving: 9

Ingredients:
a tsp vanilla extract
½ tsp lemon juice
⅛ teaspoon of salt
1 big egg yolk
1 ½ cups regular flour
¼ cup confectioners' sugar
4 oz. unsalted butter

The Custard Filling
a tsp vanilla extract
1 pound (4509 grams) fresh figs
½ teaspoon optional lemon zest
⅛ teaspoon of salt
2 big eggs
¼ cup whipped cream
1 tsp. lemon juice

3 tbsp. all-purpose flour
¼ cup of sugar
4 tablespoons melted butter

To make the Glaze
1 teaspoon honey

Method:
1. Cream the sugar and butter together for a few seconds, just until combined.
2. Mix in the vanilla, egg white, and salts well.
3. Finally, fold in the flour until well combined.
4. Make a disk out of the cling wrap and bind it.
5. Refrigerate the bread for at least 2 hours, or until it is firm enough to roll.
6. Push the flour into the bowl with your hands to lift it to the top.
7. Preheat the oven to 190 degrees Celsius. Line the cooled dough with parchment paper or plastic wrap.
9. Fill the interior of the shell with pie weights.
Cook for 20 minutes, or until the edges begin to color slightly.
11. Combine the eggs and sugars in a cup. Whisk it vigorously until it is light and soft.

12. Stir in the rice, lime juice, sugar, vanilla, and softened butter.
13. Add the cream and a pinch of salt to taste.
14. Pour roughly two-thirds of the remaining space for the figs into the partially baked pie.
15. Arrange the cut fruit as neatly as possible in the pie.
As the mixture boils, the figs will fall in even more.
16. Preheat the oven to 180 degrees Celsius and bake for 35 to 40 minutes, or until the surface appears firm.
17. Sprinkle sugar on the hot figs for a glossy coating.

Flan in Paris

Time to cook: 30 minutes
12 portion size

Ingredients:
Flan
four egg yolks
1 egg
6 teaspoons cornstarch
1 quart 35% cream
3 quarts milk
1 tsp vanilla bean
1 cup of sugar

Crust
¼ cup of milk
1 yolk of an egg
¼ teaspoon of salt
¾ cup unsalted chilled butter
1 teaspoon sugar
1 ½ cup regular flour

Method:
1. Bring the cream, sugar, vanilla beans, and peas to a boil in a saucepan.
2. Remove from the heat, cover, and set aside for 10 minutes to steep.
3. Using a brush, separate the cream cornflour in a pan.
4. Add all of the egg yolks and shells. Pour in the flavored milk slowly.
5. Cook over medium heat, stirring vigorously with a rolling pin or slotted spoon until the paste thickens and covers the slotted spoon, taking care not to scrape the plate's underside. Remove from the high heat.
6. Place directly on the milk, cover with cling film, and chill in the refrigerator or over an ice bath. Simply set aside.
7. In a mixing basin, combine the rice, salt, and sugar.
8. Insert butter and pump a few moments at a time until it reaches the width of the beans.

9. Add the egg yolk and dairy and trigger until the ball forms.
10. On a floured board, roll out the pie and cover a 20 cm (8 inch) long and 6 cm (2 12 inch) wide greased pan.
11. Place it in the refrigerator for fifteen minutes or thirty minutes.
12. Preheat the oven to 200°C with the racks at the top.
13. Spread the chilled custard over the crust.
14. Trim the surplus dough to 12 cm from the custard stage.
15. Place on a baking sheet and bake for 45 to 50 minutes or until the custard is slightly wobbly.
16. Preheat the oven to broil and emulsify for about 5 minutes, or until the custard layer is partially browned.

Bark au chocolat français

1 hour of cooking time
Size of each serving: 4

Ingredients:
½ cup apricots, chopped 1/2 inch
1 ¼ cup golden raisins
¼ cup ginger crystals
½ cup cherry
1 cup salted cashews, whole

bittersweet chocolate (7 oz.)
7 oz. Chocolate

Method:
1. Preheat the oven to 325°F. Create a 9 x
10-inch rectangular with a pencil on a
sheet lined with parchment paper board
mounted on a baking sheet, then switch the
parchment around.
2. Cook the walnuts for 8 minutes on
another baking sheet with one surface. Set
aside to cool.
3. Microwave the semi-sweet cocoa and half
of the wistful chocolate in a glass cup for
thirty seconds on high.
4. Mix with a slotted spoon. Heat and whisk
every 30 seconds until the cocoa is
completely melted.
5. Immediately add the remaining
bittersweet chocolate and let it rise to
room temperature, stirring constantly,
until smooth.
6. Pour the molten cocoa onto the baking
parchment and carefully distribute it over
the sketched rectangular.
7. Arrange the top in the following order:
ginger first, then all of the chilled
walnuts, cranberries, dried fruits, and
raisins.
8. Set aside for two hours, or until hard.

9. The bark can be cut into 18 to 20 pieces and consumed at room temperature.

Belle Helene Pears

Time to cook: 30 minutes
Size of each serving: 4

Ingredients:
8 tiny scoops vanilla ice cream
½ cup dark chocolate sauce
2 ½ cup water
4 large Bosc pears
a quarter cup granulated sugar
2 cinnamon sticks, whole

Method:
1. Gather your ingredients.
2. Combine the cinnamon sticks, butter, and half a cup of water in a small pot.
3. Bring the water to a boil, then reduce to low heat and steam for five minutes or until it is well browned and smooth.
4. Reduce the temperature to the lowest setting and gently sweep until the sugar is completely dissolved in 2 cups water.
5. Add the cooked pears to the sugar syrup solution and simmer for 15 minutes.
6. Poach the parsnips until they are fried through but not soft, measuring the

internal temperature with a knife into the thickest area of the fruit.
7. Allow the pears to settle in the liquid at room temperature.
8. Gently lift the pears from the platter with a rubber spatula.
9. Represent with a chocolate syrup rain and two little spoonfuls of vanilla ice cream.

Clafoutis with cherries

Time to cook: 55 minutes
Size of each serving: 8

Ingredients:
½ tsp. Kosher salt
granulated sugar
1 teaspoon amaretto
a quarter cup all-purpose flour
melted butter
granulated sugar ½ cup
1-quart milk
four huge eggs
½ cup cherries, tart or sweet

Method:
1. Preheat the oven to 350°F and place the butter in a 9-inch round baking dish.
2. Distribute the cherries evenly around the platter.

3. In a mixer, combine an egg and sugar until frothy.
4. Stir in the amaretto, milk, and flour mixture until smooth.
5. Pour the batter over the fruit.
6. Bake for 35 minutes until white, and a piece of wood placed into the center comes out dry.
7. Serve hot or at room temperature with icing sugar.

4.2 Traditional French Bread Recipes

Recipe for Crusty French Baguette

Time to cook: 3 hours 10 minutes
Size of a loaf of bread: 60

Ingredients:
10 oz. cold water
a little more flour
16 oz bread flour
2 tbsp. kosher salt
1 ½ teaspoons dried active yeast
1.75 oz. warm water

Method:

1. Weigh the hot water in a small cup and sprinkle the yeast.
2. Set away for the fermentation to become watery and disseminate.
3. Sift the wheat flour into a large mixing basin and whisk in the salt.
4. Make a well in the center of the dry ingredients and stir in the dissolved fermentation.
5. While mixing, slowly drizzle in the cold water until a stiff, bushy dough forms.
6. Cover the container with cling film and set aside for thirty minutes.
7. Transfer the flour to a lightly floured work surface and gently press it into a form, then cut it into quarters. At a 90-degree angle, connect the switch and the loop.
8. Place the dough in a large greased pan and cover with cling film.
9. Allow it to almost double in volume in a warm position before.
10. Divide the dough into four equal halves and shape it into a long loaf with toes pointing.
11. Place the bread on a lightly oiled towel, cover it with greased cling film, and let it double in volume.
12. Preheat the oven to 470°F and place it on a sheet pan with water.

13. Remove the baguettes from the oven and place them on lightly greased cookie sheets.
14. Using weak scissors or razor blades, make four elongated slits, one away from the other.
15. Toast the bread until it is crispy and smelly. When pressed, baguettes can produce a hollow tone.

French Bread from Julia Child

Time to cook: 8 hours 25 minutes
Size of bread loaf: 3 tiny loaves

Ingredients:
2 ¼ teaspoon salt
1 ½ cups hot water
3 ½ cups regular flour
¼ teaspoon dried active yeast

Method:
1. In a mixing basin, combine the fermentation, 212 cups of the flour mixture, and the stick blender with a flat beater.
2. Blend on medium for around thirty seconds.
3. Fill with boiling water. Begin stirring when a bushy dough appears.

4. Wipe down the beater and switch to the dough hooks.
5. Combine a few at a time in the remaining cup of flour to make a pie crust, adding more or less powder as needed.
6. Knead the dough for 5 minutes. The top should be flat, and the dough should be fluffy and sticky.
7. Turn the dough out onto a floured surface and let aside for two or three minutes while the bowl is washed, dried, and sprayed with nonstick spray.
8. Stir in the flour and let aside to rise, sealed, before 312 times its original length at room temperature. That will most likely take roughly three hours.
9. Gently flatten the dough and place it in the pan.
10. Allow the dough to rise at room temperature for 112 - 2 hours, or until it has not yet tripled in thickness.
11. Meanwhile, prepare the growing surface by rolling the flour off a baking pan onto a canvas or cotton towel.
12. Divide the mixture into three equal parts.
13. After five minutes, divide each piece of dough in half, cover loosely, and set aside.
14 Cut the loaves in half.

15. Mist the loaves with liquid. Move the loaves into the cooker with the hot oven rock and add a cup of water to the stove tray.
16. Bake for about 25 minutes or until lightly browned.
17. Spray the loaf thrice with distilled water, each for three minutes.
18. Chill for 2 to 3 hours before slicing.

Traditional (Authentic) French Bread

Time to cook: 4 hours 30 minutes
Size of bread loaf: 2 loaves

Ingredients:
1 to 2 cups warm water
1/2 cup of water
1 teaspoon yeast
1 teaspoon salt
4 c. flour

Method:
1. In a dish, bring one tablespoon of fermentation and ½ cup of lukewarm water to a boil. Simply set aside.
2. In a large mixing bowl, combine 4 cups of flour.
3. Stir the yeast mixture into the seasoned flour with a spoon, then add an additional

1¼ cups of hot water until the dough forms and pulls away from the edges of the pan.
4. Gently flour the worktop and pour it out for kneading.
5. Knead for about two minutes, or until you have a discernible ball.
6. Begin kneading the dough, however, this procedure will be different from the conventional quarter turn.
7. Pour the liquid onto the kneading sheet and straighten it with your palms to eliminate all the aerosols.
8. Divide into two sections. Place each component in a ball and rest for 5 minutes.
9. Using your fingertips, smooth out all the gases in one part.
10. Pick the top and fold 2/3 of the way back on the bread, securing it with your palm.
11. Fold and reclose. Replicate.
12. Lay flat once more, but slip back to the bottom, securing the top to the bottom.
13. Finally, shape a characteristic French bread look by softly pressing your palms with a touch of pressure along the edges of the dough.
14. Place the face of the bread seal on your sofa, leaving enough space for the loaves to stretch between the two while assisting it.
15 Cut it into three slices.

16. Cover it with the remaining towel and leave it for an hour to grow.
17. Gently peel the couch back from the loaf and place it on a baking tray or a paddle to place on the baking block.
18. Using a pastry wipe, spritz the risen dough's tips with cold spray.
19. Fill the base with half a cup of water. Place the loaf in the oven and cover with foil.

French Bread Made Without Gluten

Time to cook: 23 minutes
Size of bread loaf: 2 medium loaves

Ingredients:
1 teaspoon unsalted butter
Spray with cooking oil
1 teaspoon honey
1 tablespoon apple cider vinegar
¾ cup hot water
1 white egg
1-quart gluten-free flour
2 teaspoons quick yeast
½ tsp kosher salt
¼ cup tapioca flour
xanthan gum (¾ teaspoon)

Method:

1. Combine the grain, tapioca starch, xanthan gum, and fermentation in a mixing bowl fitted with such a whisk attachment.
2. Add the salts and swirl to combine.
3. Make a well in the center of the flour mixture and add more water, white eggs, sugar, syrup, and oil, blending to incorporate.
4. Using the stick blender, mix the paste for about a minute over a medium flame.
5. The dough will clump together. "Raise the number to be moderate and continue beating until the dough begins to adhere to the edges of the mixer bowl and appears textured," slammed.
6. Transfer the dough to a tightly covered container with a lid, shut it, and chill for thirty minutes.
7. Once the dough has chilled, place it on a level surface and brush it lightly with tapioca.
8. Lightly brush the surface of the dough with more tapioca, flip it over a couple of times, and gently whisk to clean the dough.
9. Using a large knife or bench sharpener, divide the mixture into two equal portions.
10. Work with one slice of dough at a time, lightly dusting with additional powder if necessary to prevent sticking, shaping the loaf into a form, and scratching together to secure any gaps in the bread.

11. In a quarter movement, turn the dough outward and back into it as you turn your hands away from each other along the sides of the loaf.
12. The outline should be wider in the middle and trimmed closer to the edges.
13. Place the formed rolls a few inches apart on a parchment-trimmed baking sheet.
14. Wrap it in lightly oiled cling film and place it in a heated, draft-free environment until it has grown to roughly 150% of its current length. In a dry, chilly climate, rising may take longer, while rising in a wet, moist climate may take less time.
15. Do not place it in a hot oven or raise it above a certain level since this may kill the yeast.
16. Remove from the oven and serve immediately.

Conclusion

French cuisine is currently straddling the border between Haute and nouvelle cuisine. The care that has been taken with its consistency, flavor, and beauty makes every moment special. The fact that French food is so varied is the most essential feature it possesses. Because of its careful preparation and flawless execution, French cuisine is today known around the world. It maintains great attention and devotion by portraying the normal meal as a result of art.

French cuisine has evolved through various stages, contributing to its famous standing. They refined their food into tasty, sophisticated, and fashionable dishes. French cuisine is a symbol of heritage. With this intense flavor, it's no surprise that the French stay fit, lean, and slim. Today, flavor is the most important aspect of French cuisine. With a spoonful of rich gravy, freshly caught fish, vibrant vegetables and fruits flavored with aromatic herbs; and bite-sized servings of delectable desserts, all of which are fundamental components of French cuisine. French Home Cooking is a comprehensive introduction to French cuisine and its well-known and simple dishes. Make great French meals with these recipes right now.